Page Turners

You Just Don't Know Her

Sue Leather and Julian Thomlinson

Series Editor: Rob Waring
Story Editor: Julian Thomlinson
Series Development Editor: Sue Leather

HEINLE
CENGAGE Learning

Australia • Brazil • Japan • Korea • Mexico • Singapore • Spain • United Kingdom • United States

HEINLE
CENGAGE Learning

Page Turners Reading Library

You Just Don't Know Her
Sue Leather and Julian Thomlinson

Publisher: Andrew Robinson

Executive Editor: Sean Bermingham

Senior Development Editor:
Derek Mackrell

Assistant Editor: Sarah Tan

Director of Global Marketing:
Ian Martin

Content Project Manager:
Tan Jin Hock

Print Buyer:
Susan Spencer

Layout Design and Illustrations:
Redbean Design Pte Ltd

Cover Illustration: Eric Foenander

Photo Credits:
36 Stephen Petrat/Shutterstock
37 smilewithjul/Shutterstock

ISBN-13: 978-1-4240-4648-5

ISBN-10: 1-4240-4648-3

Heinle
20 Channel Center Street
Boston, Massachusetts 02210
USA

Cengage Learning is a leading provider of customized learning solutions with office locations around the globe, including Singapore, the United Kingdom, Australia, Mexico, Brazil, and Japan. Locate your local office at **www.cengage.com/global**

Cengage Learning products are represented in Canada by Nelson Education, Ltd.

Visit Heinle online at **elt.heinle.com**

Visit our corporate website at
www.cengage.com

Printed in the United States of America
3 4 5 6 7 8 21 20 19 18

Contents

People in the story

Ash Browning
Ash is a business student at Brenton College.

Bobby Harris
Bobby is Ash's friend and roommate. He is also a business student.

Fleur Duval
Fleur is a communications student. She is very pretty and popular at school.

Dwayne Williams
Dwayne is an anthropology student and captain of the college taekwondo team.

Jenny Basola
Jenny also studies anthropology. She is friends with Ash, Dwayne, and Bobby.

This story is set in Brenton, a college town in the northwestern United States.

Chapter 1

The one

"Wow! I didn't know it was her!" said Ash Browning, suddenly.

"What are you talking about?" asked his friend Dwayne.

It was lunchtime, and Ash and Dwayne were sitting under a tree near the fountain in the college square.

"Bobby told me he met a girl," said Ash. Bobby was Ash's roommate. "But he didn't tell me who it was. Look over there."

Dwayne looked. Bobby was near the fountain with a beautiful young woman in a white dress. Bobby was smiling at her.

"It's Fleur Duval!" Dwayne said. "It's not good, Ash."

"You're right about that," Ash replied.

Everyone knew Fleur Duval. Fleur was beautiful and fun. But she was also bad news. A lot of boys really liked Fleur, and they all had broken hearts.

"You know, Tyler Jenas, he bought her lots of things," Dwayne said. "Flowers, chocolate. But she finished with him after a few weeks."

"Yeah, and what about Will Lee?" Ash said. "He gave her a necklace. He told me it was $300 or something. A week later she finished with him, too."

"She really likes nice things," Dwayne said, thinking about it.

"Yes, she does," said Ash.

Dwayne turned to Ash.

"Ash, we need to tell him."

We do, Ash thought. *But how?*

"I understand you, Ash. I really do," Bobby said. "But you just don't know her." His eyes were big behind his round glasses. His face was serious.

It was about seven o'clock in the evening, and Ash and Bobby were sitting in their room. Bobby was getting ready to go out with Fleur.

"Hey, does my hair look OK?" he asked.

"Bobby, listen to me," Ash started. He told Bobby about Tyler and Will.

"I know about that," Bobby said. "She told me. But it's different with us, her and me. I mean, I'm different, right?"

Ash was surprised. This didn't seem like Bobby at all.

"I'm telling you, Ash," Bobby went on. "She's the one for me. I know it."

"Well, listen, Bobby," Ash said. "Just don't buy her anything too expensive, OK?"

Bobby didn't answer. Then Ash saw something on Bobby's bed. It was a present.

"Hey, Bobby," Ash said. "What's that?"

It looks expensive, Ash thought.

"What's what?"

Ash asked again. "That . . . on the bed."

"Oh, well, it's a watch," said Bobby.

"You bought her a watch?"

"She saw it in the store, and she really liked it," Bobby replied. "I went back later and bought it. I mean, she's really going to love it, right?"

Ash put his head in his hands. He thought for a minute, then said, "Bobby, I'm sorry, but I need to say this. She's not a nice girl. This girl, she dates a lot of guys . . ."

"Hey!" said Bobby. "Don't say things like that!"

"OK, I'm sorry, but please listen to me. I'm your friend. I . . ."

"Just stop it, Ash," said Bobby. "I really like her. I do. And she really likes me. I know she does. And that's it. That's the only thing that's important."

That's it, all right, thought Ash. Bobby was in love, and everybody knows love makes you crazy.

"You'll see, Ash. You'll see I'm right," Bobby finished.

I hope you are, Bobby, Ash thought, but he didn't say anything.

Chapter 2

Payback

A few days later, Ash and Dwayne were in Ben's Café.

"You say he was angry with you?" Dwayne asked.

"He was angry, yeah," said Ash. "But he's . . . well, he can only think about Fleur. He's crazy about her. There's nothing we can do for him. Anyway, he's coming soon. You can try."

"Well, maybe," Dwayne said, "but Bobby has to decide for himself, right?"

A few moments later, Bobby came into the café and sat down with them.

"I need a coffee," he said.

"Bobby," Ash started. "I want to say sorry about the other day. The things I said . . ."

"Don't worry about it," Bobby said. "You were right, anyway. Here."

He gave Ash his phone. On it, there was a text message. It read:

"BOBBY, WE CAN'T SEE EACH OTHER ANYMORE. U R A NICE GUY—IT'S NOT YOU, IT'S ME. F."

"Oh, no," said Dwayne.

"The F is for Fleur," Bobby said.

"I knew that," Ash replied.

"'It's not you, it's me,' she says," read Bobby. "What does that mean?"

"I don't know," Ash said.

"Well, they always say that, don't they?" Dwayne said.

Bobby didn't stay in the café very long. Ash and Dwayne tried to make him feel better but it was no good. Bobby went. Ash and Dwayne stayed, talking about it. As they talked, they got angry.

"He spent a lot of money on her," Ash said, "and it's not like he's rich." Bobby didn't have a lot of money, Ash knew. Most evenings, he worked at the college cafeteria. His mom and dad weren't rich, and Bobby had to work. The money helped him to pay for his studies.

"You know, Bobby didn't say much, but he was really hurt," Ash went on. "I know him, and I'm telling you, he really loved her."

"I know," Dwayne said. "It isn't right, Ash. That girl is bad news."

"She sure is," said Ash.

"You know, girls like that—they meet a guy, make the guy love them, and then they finish it. She doesn't want love. She only wants to break hearts. Why's she like that, Ash? Tell me."

"I just don't know, Dwayne," Ash said. "I guess it makes her feel good. It makes her feel special, maybe."

"You know, I'd like to see the same thing happen to Fleur Duval. I'd like to see her fall in love with a guy, and then, BANG—he finishes with her. Breaks her heart like she broke Bobby's. And it's not just Bobby. Will and Tyler, too. She's laughing at us, Dwayne. She's laughing at all of us men!"

Dwayne looked at his friend. "You're right. You're right," he said. "But what can we do?"

The two of them thought about that for a minute.

"I don't know," Ash said. He put his hand through his long hair as he thought about it. "There must be someone," he went on. "Someone she'll fall in love with."

"I don't think that girl can fall in love," said Dwayne. "She just uses people."

"Listen," Ash started. "Bobby told me Fleur wants to be an actress. She wants to go to Hollywood, get in the movies."

"And . . . ?"

"A movie star. She'll fall in love with a movie star. Someone with money. Someone to help her get in the movies. She'll like someone like that. Maybe not love, but . . ."

"I don't know," said Dwayne. "She's cold, that girl."

"We have to try something!" Ash said.

"Anyway, we don't know any movie stars, Ash," Dwayne said.

"That's true."

"But maybe you have something there," Dwayne said. "Maybe not a movie star, but what about, I don't know, a movie star's brother, or cousin, or something? What about, what about the son, no, the nephew, of a movie director, something like that? Someone she thinks can get her noticed in Hollywood. Someone who can help her—someone useful."

"What are you talking about, Dwayne? We don't know any movie director's nephews either."

"No. But we can say we do. We can say someone has an uncle who's a famous movie director. She'll love that. She'll go crazy for him. Then WHAM—this someone finishes with her, breaks her heart."

"That's great, Dwayne, but who's this someone?"

Dwayne smiled at him.

"No, Dwayne. No. Are you crazy? Me? A famous movie director's nephew? I can't. No, no, no. No way."

But Dwayne just smiled.

Chapter 3

My uncle, the movie director

The next day at lunchtime, Ash and Dwayne were at the door of the college cafeteria. "OK," said Dwayne. "You know what to do."

"I don't know about this, Dwayne," said Ash.

"Come on, Ash," Dwayne said. "You're doing it for Bobby, remember?"

"Yeah, but . . ."

"It's easy," said Dwayne. "You just have to listen and say what we said, right?"

"Well, OK," said Ash.

Ash went into the cafeteria. He got a burger and looked around. Where was Fleur Duval? There she was, over near the window. She was sitting at a table with some other students. Jenny, a friend of Ash and Dwayne, was there, too. Ash walked over and sat at a different table, not far away from Fleur and Jenny.

Ash started eating his burger. Suddenly, his phone rang. He answered it. It was Dwayne.

"Oh hi, Uncle Greg," Ash said. "Great, thanks. How are you?" He listened for a few minutes. Then he said, "I see. Well, your new movie sounds really interesting."

He listened some more, and looked at Fleur Duval. He could see that she was listening. "At your house?" said Ash into the phone. "Well, thanks very much. I love Beverly Hills. And I'd love to meet all the stars from your movie. It sounds really fun. But I can't come this weekend. I've got something. Maybe some time next month . . . ?"

The call finished, and Dwayne walked into the cafeteria. He got his lunch and sat with Jenny and the others.

Fleur and the other girls were talking. Then Fleur said to Dwayne, "Hey, Dwayne, you know Ash well, don't you?"

"Yeah, sure. He's a friend of mine," said Dwayne.

"Who's this Uncle Greg he's talking to?"

"Oh," said Dwayne. "Didn't you know? It's Greg Turner, the movie director. He's Ash's uncle."

"Oh, really?" Fleur and her friends all spoke at the same time.

A few minutes later, Fleur finished her lunch and said goodbye to her friends. She got up and walked to Ash's table. "Hi," she said to him.

"Oh, hi," he said, looking up. Then he looked back at his burger.

"Umm, can I sit down?" Fleur said, smiling her nicest smile.

"Sure," said Ash. He went on eating.

"Is it good, your burger?" she asked.

"Yes," said Ash.

"I'm going to Ying-Chu's party tonight," said Fleur. "Are you going?" It was Ying-Chu's birthday, and she was having a party at Ben's Café.

"Umm, maybe," said Ash. "What time does it start?" Ash and Fleur talked for a minute or two.

"Well, I have to go to class," said Ash, as he got up. "See you later maybe . . ." He said it as though he didn't care.

Ash walked to the door of the cafeteria. When he got to the door, he looked around. Fleur was looking at him and talking to her friends.

Ash walked out. Just near the door, Ash met Dwayne. "It worked!" Dwayne said with a big smile.

"I can't believe I did that!" said Ash. *What next?* he asked himself.

Chapter 4

The date

"OK, what am I going to wear?" It was a few days later. Ash and Dwayne were in Ash's room. Ash was getting ready for a date with Fleur.

"The white shirt looks good," said Dwayne. "She'll really like you in that." The two friends laughed.

Suddenly the door opened, and Bobby walked in. "What's going on, Ash?" he said.

"What do you mean?" Ash replied.

"You're dating Fleur!" Bobby's face was angry. "Everybody's talking about it. I can't believe it. After everything you said . . ."

Ash smiled. "It's OK, Bobby. Sit down."

Bobby sat on his bed. "I don't see how it's OK," he said.

"I'm not really dating her . . ." Ash and Dwayne told Bobby about their plan.

"Yeah," said Dwayne. "It's payback time for Ms. Duval, Bobby. He's paying her back for what she did to you."

Bobby listened, his eyes getting bigger and bigger. "Well . . . OK," he said. "But it doesn't seem like a great idea to me . . ."

"Don't worry, Bobby," said Ash as he put his black leather jacket on. "This is going to work really well. You'll see!"

Ash's motorcycle stopped near the dorm where Fleur lived. Fleur ran down from her room and got on the back of the motorcycle. She was wearing a beautiful white dress. *She looks great,* thought Ash. She was a very pretty girl.

"Where are we going?" she asked.

"Wait and see," Ash said.

Ash drove off away from Brenton and got on the road to the Cascade Mountains. About forty-five minutes later, they arrived at a beautiful restaurant in a small village. The restaurant was called Bella Vista. Bella Vista had a lovely view of the mountains.

"This is great, Ash," said Fleur. "Really beautiful."

"Good," said Ash. He smiled and pulled her chair back. She sat down.

"Thank you, Ash," she smiled.

They looked at the menu. "Try the fish," said Ash. "It's very good. They get it from the river here."

They talked about college while they waited for the food. *She is lovely,* thought Ash. *I can see why Bobby fell in love with her. But I know what she's really like . . . I'm not going to make the same mistake Bobby made.*

Soon the waiter brought the food and they started eating.

"It must be really interesting," Fleur said, "having a movie director for an uncle."

This is bad, thought Ash. *She really believes that my uncle's a movie director.* Ash didn't like to say things that weren't true.

"Oh," said Ash. "It's OK, I guess. Listen, can we talk about something different?"

"Of course!" Fleur said. "I guess everybody asks you about it all the time."

"Well, yeah," Ash sat back in his chair. "Um, how's the fish?"

"You were right. This is really good." She smiled, and showed beautiful white teeth. "Really good! You know, Ash . . . I'm having such a great time. The motorcycle ride, the beautiful restaurant . . . the way you are. You really . . . You really know how to make a girl feel special."

Ash didn't know what to say. "Oh, good," he said.

"You know, most boys," Fleur said, "they just think women want expensive presents—jewelry and things."

"Oh?"

"Yes," said Fleur, smiling. "They think that's important, like they can buy your love. But love's not like that. I can see you know that, Ash."

"Really?" said Ash. He put his hand through his hair.

"Yes, really," said Fleur. "I can see that you're different."

Fleur came nearer to him, across the table.

Ash picked up the menu. "Look at the desserts. They have great apple pie here."

After dinner, they had coffee. Then the waiter brought the check. Ash looked at the check and took out his money.

"Let me pay my share," said Fleur.

"No, it's OK," Ash said. "I brought you here . . ."

"No, really," said Fleur. She took some money out. "I want to pay, too."

She's nice, thought Ash again as they got up to leave Bella Vista. *Really nice.*

When they got back to the college, Ash drove Fleur to her dorm.

"Well, thank you, Ash," Fleur said. "It was a lovely evening." Fleur looked into Ash's eyes.

"I had a good time, too," said Ash. *She has beautiful eyes,* he thought. He wasn't sure what to do.

"Ash?" Fleur said.

"Yeah?" he replied.

"Will you kiss me?"

"Sure," he said, and did.

After the kiss, Fleur looked at him for a long time.

"Wow," she said, then she went to her room.

As Ash rode his motorcycle back to his room, he knew he had a problem.

Chapter 5

The problem with love

Weeks went by, and Ash saw more and more of Fleur. He didn't see much of Bobby or Dwayne, because he spent a lot of his free time with Fleur. The two of them went for rides on his motorcycle, played tennis, and went to Ben's Café and other places around the college.

Then one day a few weeks later, Ash was on his bed with his eyes closed. He was thinking about Fleur. These days Ash couldn't think about anything or anybody else.

Suddenly, the door opened, and Dwayne and Bobby walked in. They were talking, making a lot of noise.

"Hey," said Dwayne, seeing Ash. "Here he is! Everybody's talking about Fleur Duval and you."

"Yep," said Bobby. "They say she's crazy about you. Really in love." Bobby and Dwayne laughed.

"Time to finish with her, I think," said Dwayne.

Ash sat up slowly. "Mmm . . . not now," he said. "I need just a little more time."

"What do you mean, Ash?" Dwayne asked.

Ash didn't reply.

25

Dwayne looked at his friend's face carefully. "Don't tell me you like her?"

"No," said Ash quickly. "Of course not." Dwayne came nearer to his friend. "You do, don't you?" he said. "I can see it on your face. You really like Fleur Duval!"

Bobby turned to look at Ash, too.

Ash's face was red. He didn't speak for a minute, and then, "Well, OK," he said, looking at his two friends. "I do like her, I guess . . . but she's really nice. Not at all like I thought . . ."

"What?" said Dwayne. "Not like you thought? I don't believe this."

"Well, it's true . . ." Ash said. "Maybe she didn't meet the right man before. I think she really likes me, too."

"Ash!" said Dwayne. "Remember Tyler and Will. Remember Bobby! She's bad news, my friend. You know that."

"But she's really not like that," Ash replied. "She really isn't. You just don't know her . . ."

Bobby and Dwayne looked at each other.

"I heard that before somewhere," Dwayne said.

"Ash," Bobby said quietly. "Remember that she thinks your uncle is a famous movie director, and that you go to parties with movie stars in Beverly Hills. Maybe that's why she's crazy about you."

"Yeah," said Dwayne. "If she finds out you're just you . . ."

"Oh, be quiet, you two!" Ash said. He jumped up, walked quickly to the door, opened it, and left the room.

Later, Ash went to see Fleur, and they went for a walk around the college campus. Ash tried not to think about what Dwayne and Bobby had said to him about Fleur. It was spring, and the evening was warm and lovely. Fleur looked beautiful, as always. They talked a lot, as they always did. *She likes me,* he thought. *I'm sure of it. The way she looks at me, listens to me, talks to me . . . kisses me.*

But Ash couldn't stop thinking about what Bobby had said, "Remember that she thinks your uncle is a famous movie director, and that you go to parties with movie stars in Beverly Hills." Was Fleur just with him because of his "uncle"? Because of the people she could meet if she was with Ash? He couldn't believe that. It seemed that she really liked him. *Why not just ask her?* Ash thought.

In the end, he said, "I have a question for you, Fleur."

"What is it?" she asked.

"Well," he said, "I like you very much, and I know you like me . . ."

"Yes, I do," she said, smiling. "Very much."

"But, the thing is . . . this is a silly question maybe, but do you like me because you think my uncle's a movie director, and because I spend time with movie stars?" he asked. Now he said it, it seemed really stupid.

"What?" Fleur asked. "What are you talking about?"

Ash told Fleur about the plan. He didn't say anything about Dwayne. "It's crazy," he said. "But my friend and I had this idea, that we could say my uncle was a movie director, and that I meet movie stars and all that . . ."

"But why?" asked Fleur.

"Well, just to see if people are different with me, you know," Ash said. "I know it was stupid . . ." Ash looked at her face. His own face was serious now. "But it's good to know if someone really likes you because of you," he said. He stopped talking.

"Oh," said Fleur. "I didn't know anything about it."

They didn't speak for a minute. Then they talked about something different.

About ten minutes later, Fleur looked at her watch and said, "Hey, it's 8:30! I have to go. I'm studying with Ying-Chu tonight. Bye, Ash."

She kissed him quickly and walked away.

Chapter 6

You just don't know her

"Come on, Ash," said Jenny. "You'll be OK. Really you will."

"Yeah, come on," said Bobby.

Jenny and Bobby were sitting with Ash in Ben's Café. Ash held his face in his hands. His face was unhappy. It was a month after his last talk with Fleur.

"She's not answering my calls," said Ash.

"She's just like that, Ash," said Bobby. "She's bad news. You know she is."

"What does Dwayne say?" Jenny asked.

"I don't know. He isn't here. He's at his mom and dad's, isn't he?"

"I don't think he's away," Bobby replied. "I saw him in school yesterday."

"Really?" said Ash. "I thought he was away. You know, I called him a few times, but he didn't reply."

"That's strange," said Bobby. Just then Dwayne walked in. He stood at the door for a minute.

"Hey Dwayne," said Bobby. Dwayne walked over and sat down.

"What's wrong, Dwayne?" asked Jenny. Dwayne looked like he didn't want to be there.

"What do you mean?"

"You're acting kind of strange," Jenny said.

"Well . . ." said Dwayne. "I don't know how to say this . . ." He looked at Ash. "But I think it's better if I tell you myself . . . Don't be mad, OK, but I'm dating Fleur."

"What?!" Ash, Bobby, and Jenny all spoke at the same time.

"I can't believe this!" said Ash.

"The thing is," said Dwayne, "I saw Fleur after you told her about the movie director uncle plan. She was really angry. Well, more than angry, really. She was crying and . . ."

". . . and you listened to her," Ash finished.

"You know, you really hurt her!" Dwayne said, standing up suddenly, as if he was angry.

"It was your idea," Ash told him. Dwayne sat down again.

"That's true," he said, looking unhappy.

"I can't believe this," said Ash.

"Well," said Dwayne, "you know, we got to know each other a little and we . . . well, I like her."

Ash looked at Bobby and suddenly they started laughing.

"Listen," said Dwayne. "I know you think she's a bad person. We all did. But, you see, she's not really a bad person at all. She's different. With me, I mean. Yeah, you can laugh. *We're different,* you two and me. Fleur, she's a good person. You just don't know her . . ."

Review

A. Match the characters in the story to their descriptions.

1. _____ Bobby Harris   **a.** This person is friends with Ash, Bobby, and Dwayne.

2. _____ Fleur Duval   **b.** This person has a "famous" uncle.

3. _____ Ash Browning   **c.** This person buys a watch for Fleur.

4. _____ Dwayne Williams   **d.** This person comes up with a plan to trick Fleur.

5. _____ Jenny Basola   **e.** This person is known to break guys' hearts.

B. Number the events in the order they happened (1–8).

Ash pretends to talk on the phone with his famous uncle.   _____

Ash likes Fleur and spends lots of time with her.   _____

Dwayne is dating Fleur.   _____

Bobby is dating Fleur.   _____

Dwayne and Ash tell Bobby about their plan.   _____

Ash tells Fleur the truth about his uncle.   _____

Fleur breaks up with Bobby.   _____

Ash and Fleur go on a dinner date.   _____

C. Choose the best answer for each question.

1. Why does Ash warn Bobby about Fleur?
   a. He wants to go out with Fleur himself
   b. He is concerned that Fleur will hurt Bobby.
   c. He thinks Fleur is taking up too much of Bobby's time.
   d. He thinks Bobby should focus on his work and studies.

2. Ash pretends he has an uncle who is a _____.
   a. movie star
   b. movie director
   c. rich businessman
   d. college professor

3. Where does Ash take Fleur on their first date?
   a. Ben's Cafe
   b. a restaurant in the city
   c. a restaurant in the mountains
   d. a restaurant in Beverly Hills

4. What explanation does Ash give Fleur for playing a trick on her?
   a. He wanted to impress her.
   b. He was forced to by his friend Dwayne.
   c. He wanted to teach her a lesson for hurting Bobby.
   d. He wanted to know if she would treat him differently.

5. How does Fleur break up with Ash?
   a. She sends him a text.
   b. She gets Jenny to tell him.
   c. She does not answer his calls.
   d. She tells him over the phone.

D. Write the name of the character who said the words.

1. "You know, most boys, they just think women want expensive presents—jewelry and things." _____

2. "A movie star. She'll fall in love with a movie star. Someone with money." _____

3. "She saw it in the store and she really liked it. I went back later and bought it." _____

4. "I know it was stupid, but it's good to know if someone really likes you because of you." _____

Ash Browning

Bobby Harris

Fleur Duval

Dwayne Williams

Jenny Basola

Background Reading:

Spotlight on ... *Lying*

Most of us have been lied to, or have told a lie to someone. How do we know if someone is lying to us? Researchers say there is no exact way to tell, but it's easier if you know the person well. Here are some common things to look for:

Read their body language.

Is the person avoiding your eyes?

Are they moving their arms, eyes, and hands much more (or less) than usual?

Is the person looking up and to the right while speaking to you?

Is their voice a bit higher than usual?

Do they look uncomfortable or nervous?

Read their actions.

Is the person acting different than they usually do?

Is the person more helpful than usual?

Do they get angry easily if you say you don't believe them?

Listen to what they say.

Do the details of their story change?

Does the conversation suddenly turn to things you did wrong?

Think About It

1. What are other ways to find out if someone is lying to you?

2. Have you ever found out that someone was lying to you? What did you do about it? How did you feel?

Spotlight on ... *The Chemistry of Love*

Have you ever had that "love-sick" feeling or wondered why people act so strange when they fall in love? The answer actually lies in the brain. Falling in love causes the brain to produce three chemicals (substances):

Adrenalin gives you lots of energy—and also lots of stress! This is why your heart starts beating faster when you bump into your loved one, and you get sweaty hands and a dry mouth.

Dopamine is the body's "feel-good" chemical. It serves as a "reward" for when you accomplish something, like eating a bar of chocolate, winning a competition, or kissing someone.

Serotonin helps us to sleep and eat, and keeps us feeling relaxed. Dr. Donatella Marazziti, a scientist at the University of Pisa, found that levels of serotonin in new lovers were lower than normal, which explains why you don't sleep or eat as much when in the first stages of love. Serotonin levels do go back to normal eventually, though.

A natural "love high" is produced when this mix of chemicals is produced in the brain. So, when a person is with their love, they will feel energized and happy. But, if a relationship ends or their loved one is away, the person will suffer.

Think About It

1. Have you ever been "love-sick" or felt any of the sensations described above?

2. Can you think of other activities that would cause your brain to release adrenalin and dopamine?

Glossary

actress	(*n.*)	a (female) person who acts in movies
cafeteria	(*n.*)	a student restaurant at a college
cousin	(*n.*)	your uncle's or aunt's child
date	(*n.*)	Boys and girls go on dates, such as to a movie.
director	(*n.*)	a person who makes movies
expensive	(*adj.*)	If something is expensive, it costs a lot of money.
famous	(*adj.*)	If you are famous, many people know you.
guy	(*n.*)	a man, a person
handsome	(*adj.*)	good-looking
hurt	(*v.*)	If you hurt someone, he or she feels pain.
movie star	(*n.*)	someone who is well known in movies
necklace	(*n.*)	a piece of jewelry you wear around your neck
nephew	(*n.*)	your sister's or brother's son
pay	(*v.*)	When you pay for something, you buy it.
pay back	(*v.*)	When someone does something to you, you pay them back by doing the same to them.
plan	(*n.*)	something you decide to do in the future
present	(*n.*)	something to give to someone for a birthday, e.g., a CD or book
special	(*adj.*)	If something is special, it is better or more important than other things.
uncle	(*n.*)	your mother's or father's brother